WOUNDED

ON PURPOSE

By LaKeisha T. Stevenson

Copyright © 2013 by Lakeisha T. Stevenson

Wounded on Purpose!
by Lakeisha T. Stevenson

Printed in the United States of America

ISBN 9781626970380

All rights reserved solely by the author. The author guarantees all contents are original and do not infringe upon the legal rights of any other person or work. No part of this book may be reproduced in any form without the permission of the author. The views expressed in this book are not necessarily those of the publisher.

Unless otherwise indicated, Bible quotations are taken from Holy Bible, New Living Translation. Copyright © 1996, 2004, 2007 by Tyndale House Foundation; and the Holy Bible, King James Version

www.xulonpress.com

This poetry book is intentional and the desired outcome is that you will have a tool to make it easier for you to address and discuss hard topics and areas in your life and the life of others. My hope is that you use this book as a practical tool in your small groups, residential facilities, bible studies, marriage ministries and family and friend settings. Hold on to it and share from it or seed it into the life of another to continue the chain of effective change.

This Book Belongs:

_____

Seeded to: _____ Date: _____

Seeded to: _____ Date: _____

Seeded to: _____ Date: _____

Acknowledgements

I am so thankful for my life's journey thus far and I am certainly looking forward to greater. I am thankful for the people in my life that took time to affirm the gifts that God placed inside of me that pushed me past the hurt and for those that continually hold me accountable to be my best.

To my Lord and Saviour Jesus I say, "Thank you for choosing me."

My husband Jesse, you are the greatest supporter of what God stored in me. Your love is contagious and you continue to bring out the best in me.

To Jayla, Jesse II and Master Pearson, I could not ask for a better love. You make me want to do my very best and I encourage you to do the same. I am grateful that God entrusted you to me.

My parents, Shadel and Myra Hamilton, thanks for allowing me to be and supporting my endeavors without judgment.

Pastor Herbert C. Crump, you have helped me grow in so many ways, you have a servant's heart and a leader's voice, with humility, simplicity and power. I am thankful to Lady Dawn Crump, for the spiritual counsel that helped me walk into a greater level of freedom at a pivotal point in my life. It is through you that I learned about the demon of secrecy and faced it head on.

To my siblings, Shameka, Tyrell, Shadel, Horace, LaTarsha,

Brittney, Travis and Earl, I thank you for loving me. Each of us have a special bond and I am grateful that God chose us to be a part of the same royal family. This is the season of acceleration for our lives.

To all of my special friends that stood in the low and high times, "friend" is not a loose term. I appreciate your honesty, accountability and love.

Table of Contents

Introduction vii

Chapter 1 – Affirmation 11
   I Am Who God Says I AM 13
   Every Day 15
   The Gift 16
   You Are Fruit. 18
   Queen. 20
   Free to Live 21

Chapter 2 – That Hurt Me, But... 23
   The Spirit of Violation 28
   Empty Space 34
   Speak Heart, Speak 36
   I Am Learning to Trust Again 38
   You Thought You Knew Me. 43
   Through My Loss You Used Me 45

Chapter 3 – Lovers' Lane 51
   I Wasn't Ready for This. 53
   The Connection, We Are One 55
   Love Grows. 56

The Angel	57
My Woman	58
More than Special to Me	59
My Love, My Man	60
Ready to Love	61
Recipe	63
My Hubby	64

Chapter 4 – Encouragement 67
The Shepherd	69
To God Be the Glory	70
More in You	71
Let it Rain	73
Courage	75
No Fear	76
To Encourage You	77

Chapter 5 – Life 79
The Chosen	82
Soldier Man	83
HIM	84
Near Dawn	85
Mother	87
Wonder Why	89
WORDS	91
Tunneled Vision	92

Chapter 1

Affirmation

You made all the delicate, inner parts of my body and knit me together in my mother's womb. Thank you for making me so wonderfully complex! Your workmanship is marvellous — how well I know it. You watched me as I was being formed in utter seclusion, as I was woven together in the dark of the womb. You saw me before I was born. Every day of my life was recorded in your book. Every moment was laid out before a single day had passed. (Psalm 139:13-16; NLT)

God's word was established before we ever came to be. It was and is by GOD's spoken word that we were created and yet exist. Often times in life we experience trials, tribulations, misfortunes, pains, hurt, sorrow, joy and happiness. We must be careful not to allow our existence to be defined by our ever changing emotions and visible circumstances. As important as it is not to allow negative things in your life to determine your value and worth, it also true of positive experiences. I say this because seasons change in our lives. If we build a false hope and expectation that things must go our way at all times we will easily position ourselves for frustration. "For my thoughts are not your thoughts, neither are your ways my ways, saith the LORD" (Isaiah 55:8; KJV).

There are situations in our lives that we like and some that we may not, but they all work for our benefit if we keep God first (Romans 8:28). Do not allow your life to be dictated by your surroundings, but let it determined by what GOD spoke about you before your existence. If you had a rough beginning, it does not have to dictate your ending. Some of the very things that appeared negative in our lives were some of the same things that opened our eyes and strengthened us in areas of weakness. Speak what God spoke about you before you came to this life. Death and life lie in the power of the tongue (Proverbs 18:22). Be careful of what you speak.

Learn what God spoke about you; know your heritage and rights as God's creation. Men and women were created in all shapes, sizes and races, but God said that we were created in his image. If you know that you are in God's image, then do not allow anyone else to convince you of anything else. You are great just like he created you. You are God's masterpiece!

I pray that these poems will serve as a reminder of what GOD spoke about you. Share these heart pieces with someone that may be suffering with low self-esteem, depression or an identity crisis. Speak to someone's potential and not their circumstance. Plant seeds of life so that they can be affirmed and say, "I am who God says I am!" If you do not KNOW who you are, someone will be able to tell you who you are not!

I AM WHO GOD SAYS I AM!

I am who God says I am,
Not what society tries to create me to be.
I am who God says I am
No matter my problems, history or insecurities.

Whether I walk the streets late night
Or slumped over myself from intoxication,
I am who God says I am,
Even, if my sanity goes on vacation.

I may not look like you think I should
But does that mean that
God can't use me?
Does that mean that I'm no good?

Can God not use me because my mouth is sometimes vulgar?
Can God not use me because I've committed a few burglaries?

I have slept around with a few folk
in my time,
Does that mean that God can't use me?

See, if I listen to your opinions,
points and views
I may throw up my hands!
I may say, what's the use?
But when I hear that sweet soft voice speak to me
And clearly say I LOVE YOU!

I know that **I AM WHO GOD SAYS I AM!**

The size of my hips, lips and curves
He gave them to me!
My smile, my teeth, my words
He gave them to me!

The voice that I hear is not judgmental,
Not grudgeful, but forgiving;
Not throwing up my issues
but freeing me, from my insecurities.

I AM WHO GOD SAYS I AM!

I am fearfully and wonderfully made,
He created and formed me.

I AM WHO GOD SAYS I AM!

I am his righteousness!
I am heir to the throne!
I am the head and not the tail!
I am above only and not beneath!
I am more than a conqueror!
I am the lender and not the borrower!
I **AM NOT** the life that I once practiced!
I am a sinner saved by grace.
I AM WHO GOD SAYS I AM!

Everyday

Every day I must make change
to move towards a better me.
Every day I must move past
every fear and insecurity.
Every day!

Everyday I must affirm my ability!
Everyday I must walk in his favor,
not putting off
what I can do now, for later.
Everyday I must soar with wings.
Everyday I must strive to be free.

Free in spirit!
Free in mind!
Free of my past!

Focusing on my Divine…
Divine Purpose
Divine Destiny
Every day!
I must become a better me
Every day!

The Gift

You deposited a gift inside of me,
before I ever came to be.
I lost sight of that gift and the passion
after experiencing life's tragedies.

A life of misfortune,
poverty, generational and society curses;
I was a product of my environment,
as the gift lay dormant.

I felt it kick and was about to burst;
with no visible options left
my gift was all I had.

Not believing in myself,
low self esteem, suffering abuse,
my life seemed really bad.

You loved me so much
in spite of my mistakes and failures.
You allowed people to see
my heart and show me favor.

Favor went before me,
as I started to believe.
My gift is alive and well
As I seek after my dream.

Affirmation

You made it possible and destined it to be!
My life story seemed a tragedy,
Now turned TRIUMPH
that pushed my dream into reality.

Thank you for the gift
That you placed inside of me.
When I couldn't see its purpose
You knew it would push me
to my assignment for my destiny,

My GIFT, the obstacles, the STRIFE!
My GIFT is YOUR GIFT; And your GIFT saved My LIFE.

You are Fruit

From the moment of conception the seed begins to grow
There is purpose, long before the seed was ever known.
Transformation stretches you at times beyond your limits,
or what you believe to be so,
but the stretching is one of the vitamins
that nourishes and allows the seed to grow.

God chose you because he knew that you were capable
even when you did not believe it yourself!
but remember there was and still is purpose
long before you could accept it.

Accept it, you may as well
because it makes the process a lil less strained.
God is an awesome God, He knew your purpose
long before you received your name.

So when your vision seems a lil dim
and you feel as though you are experiencing a drought,
remind yourself that you are a seed that must grow
You have purpose!
Press forward and obtain your goal!

Guess what, this thing is not just about you!
As in the natural once a seed comes forth
it is planted again, into fertile ground
to bring forth more fruit.

Affirmation

You are a seed that must become fruit
Press on, move forward!
God will see you through
Besides, Someone is watching you!

I am a QUEEN!

Born in his image,
I am fearfully and wonderfully made;
There is none quite like me.
He broke the mold
The day he breathed …
Breath into my soul

Mocha skin
Dark eyes
Round hips
Full lips
I am a QUEEN!

Every part of me was put together,
Knitted so perfectly.
I can't be shaken
For I'm his makin'

There is no other like me!
I'm his you see…
That's what make me what I be.
I am a QUEEN!

Do not be mad at me
He said the same thing about you
You gotta believe!

I am a QUEEN!

Free to live

I no longer function in mere existence.
I now walk and operate in my purpose
that the almighty God intended.

I have taken a deep breath and began to live.
I know who I am, whose I am, and why I am here!

No fear… that's not who I am.
Pure Faith!
Yeah that's me, that's how I 'm operating.

The joy is unspeakable!
I've heard that before, now I know.

I am in the land of peace, love and abundance.
No lack, because I am heir and he owns all.
Those windows have been opened
and the blessings continually fall;
spiritually, mentally, physically, financially,
Emotionally, and socially.

I am free!
I am living in my purpose, walking in destiny.
I am free to live!
I am free to be me!

Chapter 2

That Hurt Me, But...

"The spirit of a man will sustain his infirmity; but a wounded spirit who can bear?" (Proverbs 18:14; KJV)

In life we all make choices. When hurt, betrayed or mistreated, we must choose to deal with, heal from and forgive our circumstances and violator. There are times when wounds seem so deep that it is unbearable and too painful to forgive.

I must be transparent and say that there were areas in my life that I thought I had addressed and reached a point of healing. After more life incidences, I realized that there was hurt, pain and a lack of forgiveness that lied dormant within.

We must realize that anytime someone has hurt us there is a process that begins in our mind. We experience several emotions as we are coming to light of what has occurred. The transition of our emotions may include anger, pain, disappointment, fear, resentment, withdrawal, vengeance, callousness and many others. I, in some of my personal experiences, saw withdrawal first hand. My mind said, "If I remove myself from discussing what happened it will go away." Wrong – nothing can be further away from the truth.

I was carrying and covering a wound and had not confronted my issue directly. I *chose* to cover a wound! I came to the reality that it was a choice. Let's look from a practical angle: if you get a cut and it goes untreated you are at risk of an infection, resulting in a greater problem than what you began with. Covering a wound is not the best option, but I felt that my shutting down was beneficial for everyone. I took the time to consider everyone else's feelings at the expense of my own. My wound was buried so deep and because I had not seen any signs of infection I thought it was gone. As I grew in life and began to stretch, some of life's challenges hit the same area and boom! The same pain surfaced. The same area that never had the opportunity to heal was now open and oozing with infection. My infection was oozing into my attitude, my emotions and in my behavior.

Using a bandage to cover my wound did not allow it to breathe, get a scab and heal from the outside in. My bandage kept my wound moist. Therefore, I experienced the adverse effect; I was oozing infection from the inside out. At a glance, on the outside I appeared OK, but the infection was inside, that came out at the break of skin. *My healing was only skin deep.*

I was wondering, "Why?" Why do I feel like this? Why am I hurting like this? It all seemed too familiar. I found myself angry, repeating mistakes again and again, asking, *"Why?"* I was now back where I started years ago dealing with the same pain and asking questions. I remember sitting on the side of my bed, holding myself, crying asking GOD, "How can I feel the way I feel when I know that I am really in love with you?

God spoke to me clearly and reminded me of a situation that had happened in my life years before. I now realized that my issues were my reaction to my pain. I cried all of the following day and I still could not talk about my pain.

In a different conversation with one of my aunts, I remembered her telling me to forgive those that had hurt me and those that I had hurt. I had to write down on a piece of paper those that fell into that category and… I let them go. I released from my mind these pains… it was the start of a powerful process to heal in this area of my life.

Even after this I found myself yet again repeating some of my behavior, but I had to choose not to back up although it was comfortable and convenient. I had to face my issues at a deeper level.

I was at a point where it seemed like my issues and my pain were choking me; it was choking my progress, choking my relationships, choking my emotions and behavior. Once again I was at a decision point and I chose to talk this time, I *chose* to deal with the real issues.

I consulted a close friend and exposed my area of weakness. It was imperative that I trust this person enough to be totally transparent and place myself at a point of vulnerability. This individual was to hold me accountable and love me through my process. I began to discuss my inner turmoil. Honestly, I was scared and was still vague, but I was doing better than I had in previous scenarios. At least now I was bringing air to this nasty wound and cycle in my life. I knew at this point in my life that this wound healing was a matter of life and death for me. There were times that I still had to speak into the atmosphere that I forgave those that I felt hurt me.

(Breathe in through your nose and out through your mouth, slowly.)

I did something that was taboo in many of our cultures. I went to talk to a professional counselor! Wow, I was really back where I started, because 18 years prior I sat at a counselor's desk, looked at them put up a wall, became calloused and they *never* broke through... *case dismissed!*

This time was different; I was ready. I was ready to *live!* I began to release my heart, hurt, pain and issues to this Christian counselor. I did not want to cry, but I did and I needed to. What I did this time was not only name my pain, but I had to identify my violator. The demon of secrecy was removed from of my life. The enemy was now stripped of the power that he was holding over my head. *Whew!*

(Breathe in through your nose, out through your mouth, slowly).

When I chose to forgive completely, I became free! It goes back to me making the choice. I now experience inner peace. The wound was free from infection which was unresolved pain. I did not mean to hold on to the infection, but I was not sure how to let it go.

My wound is now healed, although it sometimes remains a part of the process to stay free and not let the enemy into my mind or spirit to bring up old things.

"Therefore if any man be in Christ, he is a new creature: old things are passed away; behold, all things are become new" (2 Corinthians 5:17; KJV).

That Hurt Me, But...

I encourage you to assess your situation and come to the realization of what took place. Your hurt may have been abuse of some form, failed relationships, guilt, lack of control or many other circumstances.

Today... choose to forgive those that hurt you and choose to forgive yourself. You have to start and for some it means completing the process. You may remember some accounts of your experiences, but it should only be as a reference of victory and not a tool of bondage. Your healing should display your strength.

You made it through this process so stay free; do not return to being a victim of your hurt. Use your experience as a testimony of God's power. Be led of God... someone needs to hear your story. I will attest to the fact that the same thing that hurt me has helped to birth me into my ministry. I chose to forgive!

I pray that these poems will be a blessing and a catalyst to help you in your process. I pray that they will stir healing in your spirit.

> There hath no temptation taken you but such as is common to man: but God is faithful, who will not suffer you to be tempted above that ye are able; but will with the temptation also make a way to escape, that ye may be able to bear it.
> (1 Corinthians 10:13; KJV)

The Spirit of Violation

I lie here asleep
As you rumble you hand
through my pants
Just like you're in a potato chip bag.
Touching and grabbing
As if you have some right!

I didn't invite you in
But you came anyway.

Violating my innocence!
Violating my trust!

It does not matter that I do not respond,
You continue to touch and grab
Until you are satisfied, with your hard on.

You have no right,
I did not invite you in
but you came anyway.
After you are gone
I have to deal with
"What did I do wrong?"

I walked the only way that I knew
I am a child...
I still want to play with toys and dolls.

That Hurt Me, But...

You've made me aware
Of a world that I've never known.
Now I feel emotions
and my body expresses things
that it never has before.

I don't know what to do with this!
"What am I supposed to think?"
"What do I say?"
"Who do I tell?"
You are the adult
I am only a child!

You violated my innocence!
You violated my trust!

In day light,
you want me to smile at you
As though nothing ever went wrong.
As I grow, I carry the burdens,
That you've placed on me.

I have trust issues!

Since you've touched me;
I feel like others
Should be able to.

The spirit of violation creeps in.
It drives me farther into sexual sins.

I have to battle the emotions
Because now another person is here.

Can I tell them "NO?"
I told you....
It didn't matter,
You didn't go!

So I lie here,
"I am asleep."
I don't move hoping you'll go away.
I didn't invite you in
But you came anyway.

The spirit of violation
has taken me places
That I wasn't ready to go.

Vulnerability has crept in
Now I'm sexually involved.
I promised myself that I would wait until I was married
But when faced with the opportunity;
I wasn't sure if I could say NO
Because you went places that you weren't supposed to go.

You violated my innocence!
You violated my trust!

Now I participate actively
into sexual sins.

The spirit of violation,
distrust and rejection
Has reared its ugly head.

My heart is broken
as I carry the pains of my past.
I thought I'd dealt with it
But it surfaces and I CRASH!

I lie in bed with someone,
that I have no emotional attachment.
You violated me before
And I am already here,
not sure if I can say "NO"

What did I do to bring this upon myself?
I am not sure,
I didn't do anything before…
But you came in anyway!
So I engage again, in sexual sin
Left feeling worse than I did before.

YOU VIOLATED MY INNOCENCE!
YOU VIOLATED MY TRUST!

It's not until experiences and years later
That I truly break free.
I must, because these spirits are trying to kill me.

I find myself acting out in rebellion,

I am angry and rejected.
The demon of secrecy
from carrying this burden
Has weighed heavily on me.
I must recognize what it is, call it out and be free.

YOU VIOLATED MY INNOCENCE!
YOU VIOLATED MY TRUST!

I didn't invite you in
But you came anyway.

Now I recognize and take authority of all these spirits that had a hold on me.

So I…

I denounce the spirit of violation!
I denounce the spirit of rejection!
I denounce the spirit of anger!
I denounce the spirit of insecurity!
I denounce the spirit of perversion!
I denounce the spirit of lust!
I denounce the spirit of low self-esteem!
I denounce the spirit of loneliness!
I denounce the spirit of poverty!
I denounce the spirit of being a victim!
I denounce the spirit of jealousy
And all the other things and spirits that
I… did not invite in

but they came anyway!

I invite in God's love!
I invite the Holy Spirit!
I invite Freedom and peace of mind!
In the name of JESUS
I forgive my violators.
I forgive myself.
I am healed from my past.

CHRIST you restored my value!
CHRIST you restored my trust!
CHRIST you restored me
And now, only now am I truly free!

Empty Space

As I search inside of myself
I feel the empty space
A space that was not long ago filled
For you, were in its place.

I realize that I must make an effort
To fill the void —- the empty space!
When the wind blows from the hole
God knows that I feel the chill.
The cold penetrate down to my bones.

Deep, Deep inside of me there is a warmth
That is buried by my pain
I have to clean up the mess
So that pure love may abide

The warmth and comfort
That I am in need of
Comes from my father above.

Jesus is the only one that can mend
The pieces to my broken heart
He will mend it
Make me new
And give me a fresh start.

That Hurt Me, But…

I press to search inside myself
To be whole again
The cold will be replaced soon
With the love that only GOD can give.

Speak... Heart Speak

Release, let go, relieve my mind
of thoughts and conversations.
Peace, I command it to be,
relief from the pain and misery.

Only God, only God can heal
Only he really knows how
My heart feels.

Pride, opinions and all that other stuff
can make you feel weak
but I wanna be able to listen To my heart.
I wanna hear my heart speak!

I strive to make wise decisions,
Wisdom is more precious than rubies.
I aim to make wise decisions
Not just move by emotions and feelings;
But I wanna listen to my heart
I wanna hear it speak.

Peace of mind, I command!
I must stand strong and not be weak.
A humble spirit is necessary
And a proud spirit must go.

That Hurt Me, But…

I am not able to allow ego,
emotions and surface feelings to be in control.
I wanna listen to my heart!
I wanna hear it speak

For wisdom is more precious than rubies,
it's not my battle
I have to surrender it to GOD…
Let it go.
For GOD is the captain of my ship
He's in control.

I desire to make wise decisions
I strive to do what's right.
I know I have the victory
it's not my battle
it's not my fight.

All to Jesus, I surrender
All to him I freely give.
He grants me the strength, courage, wisdom
and power to conquer and live this life that I live.

I wanna make wise decisions
I wanna do what's right.
Wisdom is more precious than rubies
I wanna listen to my heart
Speak, heart speak.

I Am Learning To Trust Again

I'm Learning to trust again
although this thang ain't easy.
I am moving from a place
where I wasn't sure who was for me
or who was against me.

The nights that I cried,
the tears that flowed,
the pain, oh the pain I felt.
I had to play in this game of life
the hand that I was dealt.
I am learning to trust again
Yal, this thang sho' ain't easy!

"I wanna be free!"
is what my heart would say
My Reply…
"Let Go, Girl you gotta let go someday!
It takes courage to "let go!"
I ask myself will I end up here again?
You see the nights I cried, the pain I felt
did not come from an enemy but from a "friend!"

So see, I had to pray!
Pray for them, and pray for me.
I am a victim of my circumstance
I could not take this thing personally!
It is not about me!.

That Hurt Me, But...

I had to tell myself so, but it was still difficult to let GO!

I don't know about you
but it seemed weird to me that the
thing that was hurting me so much
was hard to let go!
Holding on made me feel justified
For how I was feeling
I knew that I did not want to stay in this
but while I was here…
holding on almost made it feel comfortable,
If that could ever be so!
You see, I am learning to trust again!

It takes courage to move on
and past your current situation.
I knew that I wasn't enjoying this place
and certainly did not want to end up here later.

I knew that I had to make a sincere effort
so I prayed to GOD **"please do not let me have a calloused heart."**

Oh my GOD, that door was shut soooo tight
and by no means was anyone allowed in
"I am learning to trust again!"

Although there was knocking at the door of my heart I ignored it
and it seemed rude not answer when I knew
someone was standing there,
I could not bring myself to it, I WOULD NOT DARE!

I wouldn't dare act like I could hear my heart beat.
Yeah, I heard the knock
but the louder the knock, the harder I got!

The bruises, scratches and wounds
had left its mark of scarred tissue.
So now I struggle and juggle this situation in my mind
"Girl, you gotta deal with this issue!"

Once again I start to talk to myself
I had to embrace the insanity of the place that I am in.
"I know that you're learning to trust again!"
But I also knew that the price of this place
was much too steep for me to stay
"Girl you gotta let go, let it go someday."

There's the knocking…

I listen closely and slowly open the door
That's the least I could do
But you better know I only peeked my head through,
not out, with my foot posted.
I cracked the door just enough to talk
By no means was the door to my heart ajar.

I tried to talk,
that seemed to make me feel better
I was slowly making progress.

One great day I asked God

That Hurt Me, But…

to take me out of this slump
Although I knew I had made progress
I still had far to go.

I had traveled so far and was not willing to look back
I told myself,
"There is more in you!"
"There is more to you!"
I didn't want to keep it to myself but
I couldn't trust anyone enough to invite them in..
Here I go again…

"Stop adding extra drama and stress.
This person may be here to help you.
Take if for what it's worth and nothing more."

Ooh. Ooh. Ooh!
Great day!
When I let it go…Let myself free!

The door to my heart was swung wide open with my head lifted;
everything around me looked different
Now the door to my heart is ajar.

I proceed with caution and make
wise decisions
In this new place,
I'm still learning to trust, but at least I'm making moves
Picking up the fragmented pieces, Valuing my self worth.

For too long now I was making it through
Now I know I made it out!
Uh oh, watch out now!

There is laughter, where the once was sadness
there is joy where their was once pain
Now there is Peace,
when before I felt like I was going insane.
Where I felt defeat, I now walk in the victory
I'm willing to see opportunities and my abilities.
This is what happens…it happened to Me.
Through the trials and tribulation I still give God the glory.
I made it out!
Thank you Jesus, I have the victory!

So I tell you let it Go!

Start the healing process,
learn to trust again
Try at least to trust again
you will start to fly instead of feeling like a bird without wings
You will become free.

Learn to trust again!

You Thought You Knew Me!

When you walked in the door
You labeled me as conceited
But you really did not know
How bad I'd been hurt and mistreated.

No, I did not try to trust you
It's not that I didn't think you were capable
of being a friend
I didn't have time to
let my guard down and let you in.

You were already on the outside,
There you may as well stay.
I don't wanna take this risk
Because you don't know how much it REALLY took
For me to walk into this room today.

You thought you knew me…

With my great smile and positive attitude
I am making moves and pressing forward
But I know that there is much more inside of me
Some of which has not been discovered

You only see a portion of my heart
And that may not be what you like at all
I am rubbing off the callous
That came from all of the pain.

I am screaming on the inside
I wanna tell you my real name

You thought you knew me

Based on what you see
This is not my true character
But my reaction to fragmenting

Pieces... I am picking them up
and mending together.

I really am loving, passionate, compassionate, genuine
True, funny, secure, confident, anointed, driven,
affectionate, sharing, giving, and caring.

These are names that got buried under the pain
But they are screaming to come up, been down for much too long.
They want to know you, they wanna come back home.

See... you thought you knew me
much of what you saw was circumstance

I would really like to introduce myself,
You know...tell you my real name.
You need to see the true me
And as afraid as I am
I must start somewhere.

Hi, I'm _____!

Through my loss, you used me

You are excited as the news is released!
The joy that overwhelms your soul as a new mother to be.
Your body changes!
you feel the kicks of the little one's feet.

You are excited and you want to take those pictures
and hear the heart beat.
What a joy and level of expectation
Not knowing that this would end up in devastation.

"No heart beat!
What do you mean?
This cannot be!
I have purchased gifts and decorated the room
For my new little being."

All of that excitement drops
As You hear the terrible news.
Your little one has gone back to God
And not arriving to your arms soon.

All of the emotions that flood your heart;
Anger, lack of understanding and
"Lord, why me?
Why would you allow this tragedy to be?
I did what I was told.
I pray to you and live my life holy.
This was not to happen to me

because I serve you and give your name glory.

What could be the reason that I am in this space?
Lord please help me,
my heart is desolate and I have no peace.
I mean Jesus…
I still had to deliver this gift that you took from me
It seemed cruel because I got to see…

I saw the beautiful head of hair and
And the nice long fingers.
I can't believe that I can't take my child home with me.

They say that "there were complications."
You gave me no warning, Now I find myself in mourning.
Mourning the loss of what would have been
My precious…
My precious angel has gone to heaven.

God please help me because I know that you are real
And I want to feel what I am supposed to feel.
Honestly right now, I am angry and I do not understand.
Because I serve you, my faith tells me
That it was a part of your divine plan.

God I need you to make this clear to me
because I really wanted to have this baby.
I know that this had to happen for some reason
But I do not understand why.
God I am listening, PLEASE REPLY!

"My child, my child.
I know where you are and how you feel.
Remember I know what is best for you
Trust me, this wound will heal!
I had to do this, not just for you
But for the lives that you would reach out to.
I knew that you were strong enough to handle this
I knew that I could use you.

Your faith in me is strong;
And in your weakness my strength is made perfect.
There will be souls that I send in your path
That needs to hear your story.
You show that you love me so much
In your worship, praise and your ways.
I need you to trust me
and continually worship me, EVERYDAY.

The people around you are watching your response
So exemplify that you know that I am here.
Tell them that through your faith in me
Your joy has been restored!
Tell them that you did not understand
But I brought you through.
See my child this trial is not about you.

You asked me to use you for my glory.
You just didn't know how
Daughter I chose you!
I chose you for this trial.

So wipe your tears
I have put in you, everything that you need
To move through this pain victoriously.

Remember I sacrificed my own son
So I know that you can handle it,
He went to the cross for you,
So it's already done.

Tell your story.
I will give you double for your trouble.
Trust me; I know what it takes to move you to the next level.

Continually praise me, for there are others watching you.
There are many that will come to the kingdom,
Because you wanted to be used.
By your testimony you are an over comer
Your sorrow has been turned to joy
And gladness exchanged for your mourning.

My child, my child.
I know what it is you need.
I know where you are
And I know how you feel.
I let go of my son to save the lost
And through your angel,
Lives will come to the cross.

So don't see it merely as a lost

But that your angel has fulfilled
His purpose in such a short while.

Trust me, trust me!
I will restore!
Continually praise me and give me the GLORY!
I will give you double for your trouble!"

Lord please forgive me for the negative emotions.
God I thank you for making it plain
I thank you for healing the hurt and choosing me.
I thank you for being so awesome and caring so much for me.
Thank you for my angel that you sent to birth me into my ministry.
At first I didn't see it but you know what I need.
God, thank you for trusting me enough to use me!

Chapter 3

Lovers' Lane

"For God so loved the world that he gave his only begotten son that whosoever shall believe in him shall not perish but have everlasting life." (John 3:16; KJV)

The purest expression of love is exemplified through GOD, allowing his only son to die for the sins of all. God's love for us is sheer innocence! This love is unselfish! There is a Godly love that should exist between all of us, regardless of our differences or similarities. GOD desires and commands us to love one another! We cannot love one another effectively until we experience the love of Christ. Christ teaches us how to love. In Matthew 19:19 he tells us… "thou shalt love thy neighbor as thyself."

Love is multi-faceted. We will learn to be affectionate, compassionate, patient, enduring and sensitive as we love.

Love is a great and powerful gift; it conquers, it soothes, it calms, it believes and it hopes. It is easy to shadow this great gift when you have been wounded. It is through love that you will be able to move past your wound, past your hurt, past your failures and disappointments, past rejection and begin to reciprocate the love that helped you to heal. As you love yourself and others it builds confidence; you learn to listen and trust. Love is a powerful tool. Love will calm the most wounded area, the crying heart and a scattered mind. Once you experience the love of Christ, you will be effective at loving those around you. Love untainted will cause you to trust.

These poems are to bring a smile to your face and remind you of how multi-faceted and great LOVE is. This group of poems shows different expressions of love; they are a reflection of love between you and GOD, your mate, yourself and your life. I pray that you will find the words on this paper to be a message that you want to convey to your loved ones. Prayerfully you will reach a spot in their hearts and your love will grow and mature.

Love is meant to be shared in various ways and it is one of your greatest tools. Despite any scenario that has occurred in your life, you cannot give up on love. God loves us despite our errors, dispositions and history. Your heart has been made to love, but you must heal any wounds and open your heart. Love unlocks hidden treasures, covers faults and embraces hearts. If, during your reading, you find that these pieces are relevant to the lives of your friends and family, you are now commissioned to pass it on.

It takes faith to love! You have to believe to love! You must love!

I Wasn't Ready For This

Wait,
No... I wasn't prepared for this
Now I have to dismiss-the wall
That I'd set up at the door of my heart.
You have come and knocked that thang down.

Wow, I must admit
I was not prepared for this!

I find myself thinking about you
and the awesome connection;
The joy that overwhelms me
as I am in your presence.

Not trying to use any smooth words
Or eloquent speech;
You got in.

I am feeling like this
With us being at our bare necessities.

No façade.
No games at play
I wasn't ready for this
But the feelings are here anyway.

I was a lil nervous
Because it was so unexpected

I am happy, I am thankful and now
I am counting you as a blessing

I must admit…I wasn't ready for this.

The Connection, We are One!

We are one in the spirit, we are one.
Heart after God, we love and adore!
You said it out of your mouth,
I heard it in my spirit, that still small voice.
"The connection is spiritual"
Not just another religious ritual.
It's real, Oh yes I know.
We are sowers, planting so that others may grow.
Common… many things are!
Honest and real, that's some of who we are!
Passionate: certainly a characteristic;
Focused, on the same goal- Christ Jesus-the son
We are one in the spirit,
We are one!

Love Grows

Like the sunset that rises
At the break of every morning
my love grows for you.

As the flowers that bloom in the springtime
and the time changes from day to day
My love grows for you.

Like the seed that buds into a beautiful rose
Your love has touched my life,
I feel the warmth that you give, no longer the cold.

You are the shining light
That God has sent to shine upon me.
My love continually grows
You continue to make me happy.

Love…
the affection, the emotions
that it allows you to display.
I am real with you,
You are real with me
as our love blossoms every day.

The Angel

The angel that was assigned to me
Came in and loved me totally, unconditionally.

Patient, kind and true
With arms wide open
Understanding, compassionate
Saying "I simply want to love you."

"I love you for who you are
And who you are maturing to be."
I am thankful for the angel
That was assigned to me!

He has wisdom to speak into my soul,
He has the ability to love purely,
Allowing me to have personality
Without feeling that he's lost control.

My angel knows who he is
And where he stands.
My angel is Jesse
God's servant, God's man!

My Woman

For so many years now,
She has been buried
But since you have entered my life
She's resurrected.
My WOMAN…
My woman has come alive!

Your presence has brought me energy.
You have touched my woman, without a forceful entry.
I had not seen her for quite some time.
I am so elated, excited, revived!
For my WOMAN…
She has come alive.

More Than Special To Me

You are more than special to me
You are everything that I need
The beat in my heart,
The dance in my feet,
The breath that I breathe,
You are more than special to me.
You are everything that I need.

There are many that came my way
That seemed to be qualified
But they never touched what you did
Because you went deep inside.
Deep inside my soul;
Your love is pure and whole.
You are the beat in my heart
The dance in my feet
The breath that I breathe
You are more than special to me
You are everything that I need!

My love, my man!

As the sun rises and sets on the other side
My love grows and rises high,
Higher than any love experienced
Between woman and man.

Man, you make my heart go pitter patter
You, you make me slouch over in laughter.
You are the royalty, the loyalty
Oh so sweet man that I prayed for.
I did not know when I laid eyes on you…

You make my thigh twitch
My back spread
Your love goes beyond my head.
It has penetrated my heart, my mind my soul.
Your love has taken control.
My love for you grows day by day.

As the sun sets
And the light fades
The beat of my heart
Performs a parade.
I, my man, am in love with you.

Ready to love

I have some emotions,
Some feelings that lie inside of me.
I wanna be free…
Free to say I Love you
Free to say I care.
I wanna express this passion
That I feel inside,
For so long, it's been packed up,
tucked away, in hiding.

I want to share walks in the park
and cuddle on the couch.
It's been a while,
that part of my life
has been on lock down.

I don't want to share this intimacy
With just anyone
But I want to share it with you.
I wanna here you say I love you.

I need this wall to come down
I wanna be free.
I wanna be me.

I wanna love like me
I wanna hug like me.
I wanna share my sentiments

I wanna share my feelings
I wanna pamper you
I want to love you freely.

No walls, just you and I.
I am ready to love you!

Recipe

Add some sugar and some spice
I need some flavor in my life.
Soft and sensual
turn down the lights and light a candle.

Romantically involved, as I kiss your lips
A lil cayenne pepper to make it hot
I'm missing some flavor, oops I forgot.
I forgot to write a recipe
so we'll play as we go!

Improvise your actions!
you're on your way to score,
"the best lovin' award"
as I lay in your arms.

Cookin' up somethin' special
I feel safe from harm.
You add spice to my life
I'm glad you're my husband
and I'm "just peachy" to be your wife.

A bit of strawberries will add the extras
we are happily joined
as we bring one another pleasure.

My Hubby

HONEY "you do it for me!"
You are simply put, "everything that I need."
I am grateful to be your wife.
You are the love of my life.

My walk with you
has been the best walk ever,
And I look forward to
our bright future together.

You're constructive criticism, I take to heart.
You bring out the best in me
My fairytale, you've made a REALITY.

You know my ins and out
And what it takes to pull me
To the next level.
Our covenant has been tested
But it has indeed made us so much better.

I am blessed that you are my king!
I am elated to be your Queen!
You are an awesome provider.
You are an excellent father.
I am blessed to walk this path with you.
Your wisdom and heart for GOD
Continues to reveal things fresh and new.

I am overwhelmed by your passion,
Tenderness, attentiveness and love.
Thanks for listening and also hearing me.
I never knew what love truly was
Until YOU…

The priest of my home,
The beat of my heart,
The lover of my life came to me.

You… made my dreams a reality
And I my love, my friend am blessed to have,
YOU!

Chapter 4

Encouragement

Seasons come and seasons go; life must continually move on. There are challenges that groom us to become our best even if we cannot see the picture initially. When you are in the middle, be encouraged. Do not fear because God knows where you are and what you need before you have need of it. There is no point or season in your life that catches God off guard. In your roughest moment remember that the bulk of the word through is "rough". You must stick to it and hold on.

If you are truthful and reflect on some of your most trying moments you will say "I learned something" – either things to do or things not to repeat. God does not allow the storms in our lives to overtake us; he allows them to prune us and have us effective for our God-intended nature. God created us good… along the path of life we have picked up things that may not have been for the journey. Through these defragging and reflective moments we can come into proper alignment and posture, our faith will grow, we have a testimony to be effective witnesses and God will be glorified and his people edified.

David was a man after God's heart and he encouraged himself. He knew that the things he endured and overcame were beneficial for his development. David said, "It is good for me that I have been afflicted; that I might learn thy statutes" (Psalms 119:71; KJV). There are times that we do not feel like doing things because of the pressures of life, but I do not want you to be led by your emotions, but be led by the promises of God. Speaking the word of God over your life in your matters will cause your flesh to come into alignment with what your spirit knows. Your spirit knows that you are more than a conqueror and an overcomer because that is who God created you to be. Your spirit knows that defeat is not an option, but you have to confess to your mind that you choose to stand and live on these principles. It important to fill your mind and space with positive influences and conversations; healthy declarations and associations are vital to healthy living.

> I pray that these choice selections will serve as an encouragement in your process of life. Seasons come, but they do change. It takes the sunshine as well as the rain, the good and the bad, the test and the victory to live a balanced life. Encourage yourself no matter what state you are in. "In all things give thanks, for this is the will of God concerning you in Christ Jesus" (I Thessalonians 5:18; KJV).

The Shepherd

When you must make decisions
That seems to be the most difficult
Stand on what you know
And not how you feel.

Not allowing your emotions to get the best of you
Knowing that the facts ARE THE FACTS
And the truth is real.

When your back is against the wall
And standing against all manner of test
Choose the God decision
Knowing that your decision affects the rest.

You are the Shepherd of this house
The guide of the fold
Honor the GOD head!
Be spirit lead!
And we can't go wrong.

To God be the Glory

Every opportunity that the enemy has
To convince me that I am not worth it,
He takes a shot.
Everything that God says I am
He says I am not.

What he doesn't realize
Is that my life is not in his hands
And for every attack that he wants to launch on me
He must ask permission.

If the master says yes, then it's a part of the master's plan
So… accept what God allows
And give him the glory that is due his holy name.
No glory to the enemy, he meant it for bad
And GOD made it good anyway.

Truthfully, if the enemy knew that his attack would bless you
He wouldn't have tried.
God allows the trials to make us
Even though there are times when it feels
As though we are dying.
To live in Christ, I must die to my flesh!
Go through my brother, my sister
Pass the test.

More In You

There is more in you
And you know this to be true
But you fell into a slump
And it seems like you've been lying down…
Looking up

MEDIOCRITY…

Will afford you the best opportunity
To stay where you are

COMFORT…

Is a first class ticket to misery.

Why You ask?
Because…
If you do not set your goals
On something higher
Then you don't have to reach.
You become complacent
And will not stretch beyond your point of comfort.

Performing a task is one thing
But performing with excellence
Is an entirely different game.

REACH!

Beyond your limits
It will stretch you
And you will live up to your name.

There is more in you!

Let it rain

I thank you for the rain
That is pouring into my life;
For after the rain, there must be sunshine.
The rain will water the crops
In this case, the seed; so that it will grow.

It may seem a lil dreary
As you are driving through
But remember it has to rain.
Keep in mind seasons come
But they must change.

The struggles… consider them rain
But your victory and overcoming
Is the sunshine.

Consider your weakness, rain
But the power and strength through the holy one
Is the sunshine.

Your setbacks, consider them rain
But you're coming forth with power and zeal,
This is the sunshine.

Have you ever seen the sun shining
in the midst of the rain?
Yes, that is when it produces a beautiful rainbow
The little folk's tale says

"on the other side there's a pot of gold."

It's you!
You are the pot of gold on the other side of the rainbow
So let it rain!

Smile through the rain
Smile through the storm
You are coming forth as pure gold.

The rain will wash away the dirt
That lies on the foundation of your heart

If you have to cry, do what you must
The tears are your rain.

Let the rain wash you
But when the sun comes out
You won't be scorched
And you will blossom.
Blossom into a golden flower
So let it rain!
Let it pour!

You have not seen
What God has in store
Let it rain,
It's watering your seeds
Let it rain!
Showers of blessings, let it rain!

COURAGE

Courage!
Why?
Because he has not given me the spirit of fear
But of power, love and a sound mind.

Courage!
Because he spoke a word for my life
Prior to my existence among mankind.

Courage!
Because he called me!
I am chosen …
To be the head and not the tail,
To be above only and not beneath.
I am of a royal priesthood!

Courage!
For I have power to tread on serpents and scorpions
After the holy ghost has come upon me.

Courage!
Just because he is GOD… and I am his.

No Fear

No fear!
I cannot operate like that anyway.
I am apprehensive in my human nature.
I do not know what to expect.

Things are not what they use to be
This is certainly unfamiliar territory.
I know that there is a purpose for me being where I am
At times, I feel strength
At others, I feel weak.

I have to coach myself!
This is unfamiliar territory.
I need directions to my DESTINY PLACE.
I am going and I know…
Some things I expect and others,
I don't know what to…
Even with uncertainty I must operate with NO FEAR!

Encouragement

<u>To Encourage you…</u>

This place is unfamiliar and certainly not comfortable.
You can handle all that is coming at 'cha!
Not because the times aren't trying
but because of what has been placed on the inside of ya.

Strength, courage and wisdom
has been developed, from the previous trials.
Your winner instinct says
"Everything **will** be alright."

In the fleshly vessel we all get tired sometimes
that's when I have to be who I am
hold up your arms and encourage you to fight.

Be encouraged because the lord knows exactly where you are
Everyone's path is different and sometimes our road seems hard.
There is Greatness inside of you, so the trials seem to have a lil more thump
Keep in mind whose you are and that every battle is already won.

Your destiny is in place and you must keep marching towards it
The stuff in the middle is pushing you there,
even when you don't understand it.
You are powerful, You are strong, You have favor
and the promises are manifesting.
I have confidence in GOD that you are so close to your blessings.

KEEP your eyes open and stay focused on his word
though the vision has an appointed time; it shall come forth;
will not prove false and shall not lie!

Don't let your surroundings fool ya
See what you **heard** GOD say!
Stay focused, it's close.
I know that you can feel it.

BE ENCOURAGED

Chapter 5

LIFE

"You did not choose me; I chose you and ordained you that you should go and bring forth fruit; fruit that shall remain that whatsoever you ask my father in my name he will give it you." (John 15:16; KJV)

Your path has been ordered! You did not get the opportunity to choose your race, your gender, your parents, your family or the neighborhood that you came home to; they are all a part of the life that you've been given. God knows all about you and what his assignment is for you. There are some choices that we make, but the fact that God chose you is non-negotiable; you can make that choice easy or hard. I think about Saul; he was chosen. Even when Saul was persecuting the church, he was still chosen. He could have chosen not to surrender, but he did surrender to the voice of God. Saul's name was changed to Paul and he was one of the most influential apostles in the Bible.

It does not matter where you have been or what you have done. It is by grace, through faith that we are able to live a holy life before GOD. We have been called with a holy calling and Jesus sacrificed his life so that we can live. Do not kick against the pricks; choose to hear the voice of God that calls you. Your life is not your own! You were made fearfully and wonderfully and for God's own purpose and good pleasure. We deal with many people on this journey; no matter what your role is JESUS has to be the center.

This life can be great; you have to walk in the destiny that Christ has intended for your life. Choose Jesus; he chose you. His choosing you does not negate the fact that you will face obstacles and trials. Quite the contrary; his choosing you means you may face some rough times because he has his seal of approval on you and has given you everything that you need to be victorious and overcome any situation. His choosing you may sign you up for things that you of your own accord would never opt in for. In this life things that we face help us to learn much about ourselves, our strengths, weaknesses and those of others. It is important to remind yourself that you are chosen because when the waves and storms of life hit, it may not feel like it, but there is always a purpose. There will be many emotions and feelings that you face, there will be laughter and sadness, there will be questions and answers, people may change in your life, but the overall outcome is that you are a winner.

A life submitted to God will help you to deal with this world that you live in, but as a believer of Christ you must set your sight on things of the spirit and not rest in carnality.

You did not create your life, so as you live it, trust the one that gave it to you.

Allow your life to be defined by the name that God calls you. In this life with Christ you are more than a conqueror and you have a confirmation through the Holy Scriptures. A life submitted to God will yield you the productivity, fruitfulness and peace of God despite the matters that you will face. I challenge you to see others the way that God desires you to view them. All of us along with our differences and similarities help to maintain balance. Your view of life will affect your quality of life. Make it a personal goal to live and not simply exist.

The Chosen

The chosen does not have an option
But a mandate on his life.
You must live holy!
Gotta live right!

Ya' see he chose you that you will go and bring forth fruit;
Fruit that will remain.
To bring his name glory
And save the lost from their sin.
You are chosen and you have a responsibility…
To live right, to live holy.
You must bring our father, his due glory
HE chose **YOU!**

The Soldier Man

Arms of steel
Heart of Gold
so selfless to sacrifice
your life for our country
and our "personal" world.

Courage to take on problems
that you did not create.
Strength to fight in the desert
eat bugs, be uncomfortable
and stay up late.

We appreciate your existence,
resilience, discipline and wisdom.
Keep your focus and God in first place
Return home to us and be proud
of what you have fought for.

Come home soldier man, come home!

HIM

Man!
Strong, wise, smart and powerful.
He is the start of my existence.
If I understood his position
then I would appreciate his existence.
I cannot do what he does
because it's tailor made for him.

Look at him!
Speak to his worth!
Speak to his value!
Speak to his potential!
Respect the man in your life, build him up, comfort him,
touch his heart and help to heal hurt.

God ordained him to lead as he follows Christ.
Esteem the man in your life;
husband, father, brother, co-worker or friend.
Build strength, en.courage leaders, esteem the man in your life.
Love HIM!

Near Dawn

New lyrics, for a brand new song
The hour seems kind of dark.
It's almost near dawn.
Still dark, I can see the shadowing from the moon
But the sun is coming up.
It must be near dawn.
The sun must shine soon!

Rain, rain go away
Come back another day.
It will rain and it may even storm
But ya still must know
It's almost near dawn.

In the rain, the blessings are showering
The crops are being watered
The roots are taking hold
And the leaves are blooming.
It must be near dawn
But it still seems so gloomy.

Which crop will stand through the rain?
Some will die
And some will strive to live
But with great strain.

If you survive this storm
You'll know how to prepare for the next.

You'll push up through the ground
And be one of the best.

Others are being picked
And it seems you're overlooked
But it's still not your time
Or season to come forth.

The journey has been tough
And night appears so long.
It comes before the break of day
Oh my gosh, It must be near dawn.

Mother

Wow, Where do I begin?
She is a wonderful mother, grandmother, baby sitter and friend.
Woman of Elegance, class and skill.
"Nurturing" should be her middle name,
Determination is a driving force!
As strong as a lion but as cuddly as a kitten
Her courage and strength could never be duplicated
And certainly should never be underestimated.

Her faith in God has allowed her to raise a beautiful family
Especially me!
I could never repay her for her wisdom
For she taught me in her actions
As well as in her deeds;
She is always careful to consider
When others are in need.

Success has laid at her feet
She always remained graceful and walks in humility.
Unconditional love has always been displayed
She is a positive role model
And great values were instilled.
I have said all of this
And she has not even made it over the hill.

Her smile is vibrant, her touch is warm
She is my mother
A valuable and priceless jewel!

A woman of strength, courage and wisdom,
Unselfish, devoted, caring, loving and sharing;
The epitome of integrity!
Mother you are my charm,
These are a few things that I could say
To express what you mean to me.

Wonder Why?

Why are you ignoring me?
Can't you hear me speak?
No, because you don't understand me
You think I'm soft and weak.

You can't know because you've never been.
You've never been where I am;
So you can't imagine from where I came.
But you sit and stare at me
With disgust and shame.

Ashamed... Ashamed of what?
How would you know?
You sit high and think
That I am so low.

To low for you to recognize
But you're not better
Cause I'm rising to the top!

When you look down on me
You're keeping yourself down
That's why I dare not
Lose my joy or smile.

It's just a season, a trial, a test
Sit back and watch me rise
Rise to be my best.

Wounded on Purpose!

As I come up
I won't push you down
I'll help you climb
And we'll both receive our starring crown.

You still look at me and wonder why?
Why I helped you climb
It's because I have power, love and a sound mind.

I won't be a victim
Of not being able to forgive
Because if I forgive
I earn more power and strength to live.

And you still wonder why!

Words

"You can't make it!"
"If he loves you why must you take this?"
These are the words of the enemy
I must stand up boldly and tell him…

"It is a test of my faith
A test of my strength
A testimony of how I defeated you
With God, all things are possible"

"Lord,
I can do what you say I can do
I will be what you say I am
I will go where ever you send me
Because…
With you God, all things are possible"

Tunneled Vision

Is it really the way you see it?
Or do you have a narrow view
Open your eyes see the glory
There is still more to you.

You know that you are not
What they say you are
Or who they say you'll be
But what you have is greater
Than the narrow view will allow others to see

No! Don't look for acceptance
Or for them to be happy, with your success.
Their vision is tunneled
And he thinks it makes him less;

Less of a man, woman, boy or girl
But the difference between you and them
Is that you realize it's your world

It's what you make it
And what you've worked for
They don't know how you got here
But their aiming to pull you down,

Be not afraid
For when they rise up against you
They shall stumble and fall.

CPSIA information can be obtained at www.ICGtesting.com
Printed in the USA
BVOW030547010513

319545BV00001B/2/P